GUY BILLOUT

SOMETHING'S NOT QUITE RIGHT

RIGHT QUITE NOT SOMETHING'S

David R. Godine, Publisher · Boston

First U.S. Edition published in 2002 by

DAVID R. GODINE, Publisher
Post Office Box 450
Jaffrey, New Hampshire, 03452
www.godine.com

Simultaneously published in France
by Éditions du Seuil as
Y a encore quelque chose qui cloche
Copyright © 2002 by Éditions du Seuil

LIBRARY OF CONGRESS
CATALOGING-IN-PUBLICATION DATA

Billout, Guy
Something's not quite right / Guy Billout. — 1st edition
p.   cm.
ISBN: 1-56792-230-9 (alk. paper)
1. Billout, Guy — Catalogs — Juvenile literature
2. Paradox in art — Catalogs — Juvenile literature
I. Title
NC975.5.B53 A4 2002
165—dc21 2002026383

First printing
Manufactured in France

THE END